The Early Americas

Contents

Civilization 2
Reference: Dictionary

Come to the Native American Festival 4
Nonfiction: Newspaper Article

Mayan Math 6
Nonfiction: Fun Facts

Mayan Song of the Earth 8
Traditional Chant

Diary of Hernando Cortés 10
Fiction: Historical Fiction

The Conquistadors 20
Nonfiction: Description

Hoof Prints in a New Land 26
Fiction: Fantasy

El Tikal Restaurant 30
Functional Reading: Menu

Writing Model: Report 32
Purpose: To Explain

Index 33

Rigby

ꞁ i pin ꞁ a face ꞁ ə = e in happen ꞁ

civilization

(siv'-əh-ləh-**zā**'-shən)

noun. a society that has government, farming, and trade

Come to the Native

by Jaime Fatás, NEWS Staff Writer

Plains Indians wear special clothing during a dance.

Native Americans from around the Northeast will gather this weekend at the annual Native American Festival at Bennett Park. A Powwow is set for 2 P.M. Saturday.

Newspaper Article

American Festival

October 14, 2004

At the festival, Native American artists will show their crafts. Storytellers and dancers will put on a show.

Basket weaving and other crafts will be displayed at the festival.

Mayan Math

The Maya have lived in Central America for thousands of years. They invented many things, including their own number system.

1 •	2 ••	3 •••	4 ••••	5 ▬
6 •/▬	7 ••/▬	8 •••/▬	9 ••••/▬	10 ▬▬
11 •/▬▬	12 ••/▬▬	13 •••/▬▬	14 ••••/▬▬	15 ▬▬▬
16 •/▬▬▬	17 ••/▬▬▬	18 •••/▬▬▬	19 ••••/▬▬▬	20 ◈

How to Read Mayan Numbers

Read the number from bottom to top.

• = 1

▬ = 5

Try a Little—Learn a Lot!

Here are some math problems that use Mayan numbers. Use the table on page 6 to solve them. Check your answers at the bottom of this page. Then make up a few math problems of your own.

A. ⟍ + ⟍ = ?

B. ••• + ⟍ = ?

Fun Facts

> The Maya invented the idea of zero, or none.

> The Mayan system counts by 20 instead of 10.

Answer Key

A. ⟍ (6 + 8 = 14)   B. ⟍ (3 + 9 = 12)

Mayan Song of the Earth

adapted from the *Popul Vuh (1554–1558)*, an
ancient Mayan text

Measured is the time when we can
Praise the splendor of the earth.

Measured is the time when we can
Know the kindness of the sun.

Measured is the time when the blanket
Of the stars looks down upon us.

And through time, the shadows,
Living within the stars,
Keep watch over their safety
And take measure of their fate.

Diary of HERNANDO CORTÉS

by Jared Matt Greenberg

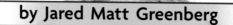

February 18, 1519

My dreams of adventure in the New World may come true now! We set sail for the Yucatán Peninsula today. I may never see my home again. I am excited and a little nervous.

I go seeking bigger and better things—
a chance to become a hero, and most of
all, to get rich! The native people say there
is much gold in a place called Mexico.

H.C.

NORTH AMERICA

ATLANTIC OCEAN

Gulf of Mexico

CUBA

HISPANIOLA

YUCATÁN PENINSULA

Tenochtitlán

Caribbean Sea

Key

Aztec Lands

Route of Cortés

March 14, 1519

We met the Tabascan people. At first we fought with them, but then they offered us gifts of peace—a lot of food, some jewelry, even a few roses for our horses to eat!

H.C.

August 16, 1519

The Aztec rule this land. Today we met some of their people. They have much gold! The Aztec think I am a god called Quetzalcoatl. If they think I'm a god, maybe they will give us their gold.

H.C.

November 8, 1519

We have traveled with the Aztec to their capital, Tenochtitlán. We met the Tlaxcalans, a people who have long been at war with the Aztec. The Tlaxcalans are willing to help us fight the Aztec if there is a war.

H.C.

November 24, 1519

Tenochtitlán, the Aztec capital, is the most beautiful city I have ever seen! The Aztec think I am a god. They treat us like kings. Today we will kidnap their ruler, Montezuma, and ask him for gold.

H.C.

July 1, 1520

What a horrible night! The Aztec have taken over the city. They are angry that my reckless captain, Pánfilo Narváez, killed many Aztec chiefs while I was away. We tried to sneak out, but the Aztec heard us and trapped us in the lake. We have lost 850 soliders, 4,000 Tlaxcalans, and most of our treasure!

H.C.

April 28, 1521

We are ready to attack Tenochtitlán again. This time, we have boats and a whole army of Tlaxcalans. If the new Aztec ruler won't accept my peace offer, we will go to war with him.

H.C.

August 13, 1521

   We have been fighting for 75 days. Tenochtitlán is crumbling. The Aztec warriors are too weak to fight. Today we captured their ruler. The Aztec have fallen! I am now ruler of a territory that stretches from the Caribbean Sea to the Pacific Ocean. The glory is ours!

H.C.

January 15, 1524

My dream has come true. I am the governor of New Spain—all the land Spain controls north of the Isthmus of Panama. A new city stands on the ruins of Tenochtitlán. We will call it Mexico City. What a glorious new adventure!

H.C.

The Conquistadors

by Denise M. Jordan

They came from a nation of adventurers. They traveled the globe to find land and riches, and they changed the world forever. Who were they? They were the conquistadors, Spanish soldiers who conquered new lands over 500 years ago.

Exploration of Early Americas

The conquistadors sailed to the New World in giant ships. Each ship had three thick masts and wide sails.

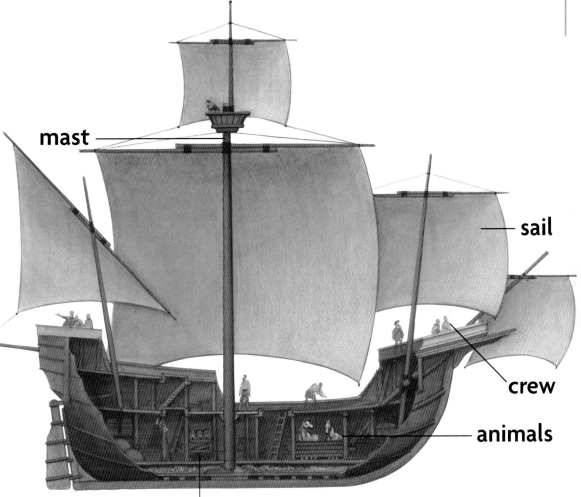

mast

sail

crew

animals

supplies and weapons

1500 | Conquistadors begin exploring the New World.

In what is now Mexico, Hernando Cortés conquered the Aztecs and took their gold and silver. The Aztecs had a giant calendar made out of gold, thick gold chains, and bright jewels. Cortés built Mexico City on the ruins of the Aztec capital.

Aztec calendar and gold jewelry

1521 | Hernando Cortes conquers Mexico.

Hernando De Soto and Francisco Pizarro sailed to South America and traveled into the jungles of Peru. They marched into the Inca capital, killing the Peruvian ruler and making slaves of the people.

1531–33 | Hernando De Soto and Francisco Pizarro conquer the Incan Empire.

In 1540 Francisco Vasquez de Coronado searched what is now New Mexico and Arizona. He was looking for the Seven Cities of Cibola. According to a legend, Cibola's streets were paved with gold. Coronado was disappointed to find only a village of stone houses.

1540 | Francisco Coronado explores Arizona and New Mexico.

As Spanish men settled in the Americas, they moved into local towns. Some married local women. Soldiers and priests taught the Native Americans many Spanish customs. However, the Native Americans also taught the Spanish many important things.

New Foods, New Ideas

The Native Americans introduced the Spanish explorers to foods such as sugar, corn, and potatoes.

1550 | Spanish settlements spread across the Americas.

Hoof Prints in a New Land

by Helen Strahinich

The wind whips my mane as I gallop across a grassy plain. I kick my legs with joy to feel the earth beneath them. We spent many months at sea on a noisy, crowded ship. There were hundreds of us crammed into a few pens.

Now we run free! We are the first of our kind here. The soldiers have set up camp, seeking land and treasure. They haven't put us inside fences, but they always keep an eye on us.

De Soto and Horses

Hernando de Soto brought horses to explore the land that is now Florida. He discovered the Mississippi River.

I stopped to eat grass in the field. Some strangers passed by on foot. "Who are they?" I wondered. They looked different from the soldiers I knew. I found out by following them.

The strangers came to a village. One girl put out corn for me and soon I began to trust her. Each day she came closer. Finally, I took the food. Then I stayed with them.

Native Americans and Horses

Some Spanish horses got away. The native people tamed them. These horses changed their lives.

El Tikal Restaurant
A Taste of Guatemala!

Main Dishes

Arroz con Pollo Chapina *(Chicken and Rice)*

A casserole with chicken, rice, tomatoes, carrots, olives, and green peas

$8.95

Jocón *(Chicken in Green Sauce)*

Chicken fried in a sauce made with cilantro and green peppers

$8.50

Carne en Adobo
(Beef in Tomato and Pepper Sauce)

Boneless beef simmered in a sauce made with onions, tomatoes, and red peppers

$9.25

Tamales Negros *(Black Tamales)*

Cornmeal filled with a mild chocolate sauce and choice of chicken, pork, or beef

$3.25 for each tamal

Salads

Picado de Rábano *(Radish Salad)* $2.75

Iguashte *(Vegetable Salad in Squash Seed Sauce)* $3.50

Beverages

Jugo de Coco *(Coconut Juice)* $1.25

Ponche de Frutas *(Fruit Punch)* $1.50

Mr. Pablo Ruiz and Ms. Maria Ruiz, owners

The Mexican Flag

The Mexican flag stands for Mexico's history. The green stripe represents hope. The white stripe represents honesty. The red stripe represents family. The middle of the flag shows an Aztec legend. Legend says the Aztec settled where they did because they saw an eagle on a cactus eating a snake. They thought this was a good sign. Today, Mexico's flag reminds people of their history.